Red Sandstone Buildings of Edinburgh

MALCOLM MACNICOL & MICHAEL DEVLIN

Red Sandstone Buildings of Edinburgh

No city is vibrant if it does not develop. The bright red sandstones of the South of Scotland, introduced in the late 19th century, were certainly a shot in the arm for the City of Edinburgh. Their arrival caused quite a reaction amongst some of the residents. Set against the paler yellow and grey sandstones indigenous to the city, the contrast could not be plainer. So, as with the application of innovative architecture and design, the use of contrasting material can shock, please and displease in equal measure.

But no one can deny that the 'romantic intrusions', as the authors of this volume describe them, have provided a wonderful legacy of part of the Permian to Triassic geology of Scotland – a sort of 'homecoming' of stone to the Capital. There is little question that during these geological time periods, the desert environment extended across much of the land. Today's sedimentary basins of Dumfries and Thornhill, Lochmaben and Moffat, Mauchline, Arran and Stranraer, are but fault-preserved remnants of a much more extensive deposition of sediments laid down by both wind and water.

Evidence from the rocks indicates that the trade winds which brought much of the Permian sand to Scotland originated from the east. It seems appropriate that the very name Permian was coined in 1841 after Permia, the central Russian province, by Sir Roderick Murchison, a Black Isle man who travelled far. Triassic derives from a three-fold division of the rocks recognized in Germany. The original name Trias was proposed in 1834 by German palaeontologist Friedrich August von Alberti. So Scotland's Permo-Triassic red sandstones are just part of the global story. Because they form such fine building stone resources, the public may readily observe the geological features embedded in our buildings and monuments.

This book is indeed a celebration of red sandstone in the City. Look closely at these superb photographs and you will discover geology's code of sedimentology and mineralogy which unlocks a fascinating story of Scotland's past environment of 200 to 299 million years ago. See also how architects of several generations have imaginatively employed this versatile natural material. The authors are to be congratulated for opening our eyes to buildings that we walk by every day, take for granted even, but which provide the spectacular backdrop to a beautiful city.

Andrew McMillan, Geologist
British Geological Survey, Edinburgh

Fig 1: Sweetheart Abbey was completed in the 14th century.

Red Sandstone Buildings of Edinburgh

Anyone who lives in or visits Edinburgh will notice the romantic intrusions of her 'new' red sandstone buildings, truly a city within a city. From churches to pubs they draw attention to themselves, redheads amidst the blondes, brunettes and greying tones of the older town (Youngson 1966). As with all substantial and carefully wrought structures they provide the urban skeleton upon which both the form and function of the Scottish capital depend. This short book hopes to reveal them afresh: 'the curtain rises and the scene is set' (Miller 1841), for this rich heritage daily provides a fascinating 'open-air museum of quarry products' (McMillan et al 1999).

The churches rejoice in their pertinent asymmetries, ringing the city with elegant appeal at Colinton, Craiglockhart, Polwarth, Greenbank, Cluny, Morningside, Gorgie, Bristo, Restalrig, Inverleith, Comely Bank and Dean. Congregational transactions and amalgamations within the Kirk have resulted in changes of name in many instances (Smith 1979) but the beauty of these buildings is unaltered. From the ecclesiastical to the secular, the implacable fortifications of the Caledonian Hotel and the King's Theatre protect the western approach from mischievous Glaswegian incursions. Centrally, the palatial Gothic of the Scottish National Portrait Gallery flaunts figurines, lofting parapets and pinnacles while the Dean Village in its historic gorge plays a domestic but romantic role.

Around the Meadows' edge are found the busy sites of the Royal Hospital for Sick Children, the Fire Station and Edinburgh College of Art, the old Royal Infirmary with its Jubilee Pavilion and the Warrender Park Free Church (both now residential), and the Church Hill Theatre. The rouged taverns of the Golf, Athletic Arms, the Abbotsford and Robertsons 37 Bar in Rose Street, the Greenmantle, the Morning Glory, and the Foot of the Walk and the Rosekeith in Leith are sternly counterbalanced by the grandly crow-stepping former Castlehill School with its scholarly following of educational establishments at Bruntsfield, the Canongate, Leith, Roseburn, Boroughmuir by the Bruntsfield Links, and South Morningside. The Currie and Stockbridge schools have translated themselves into libraries while in the middle of Princes Street the douce old Edinburgh Café stands tall, squashed between some regrettable modernities.

Confident residential tenements, terraces and town houses expose architectural quirks in the familiar suburbs of Morningside, Braid, Polwarth, Marchmont, Blackford, Portobello, Leith, Inverleith, Roseburn and Murrayfield (Gifford et al 1991; Cant 2001). Ramsay Garden camouflages its subtleties and delectable 'ice-cream confection' (McKean 1992) below the Castle esplanade, from where red sandstone detailing spreads down the Royal Mile and across all sectors of the city.

The quarries that supplied these rust and pink landmarks provided stone locally in the Dumfries and Annan regions from the 14th century (Hawkins 2001), the most ambitious project being the construction of Sweetheart Abbey (fig 1). By the 1850's quarrying and stone preparation were engaging

Fig 2: Locharbriggs quarry today.

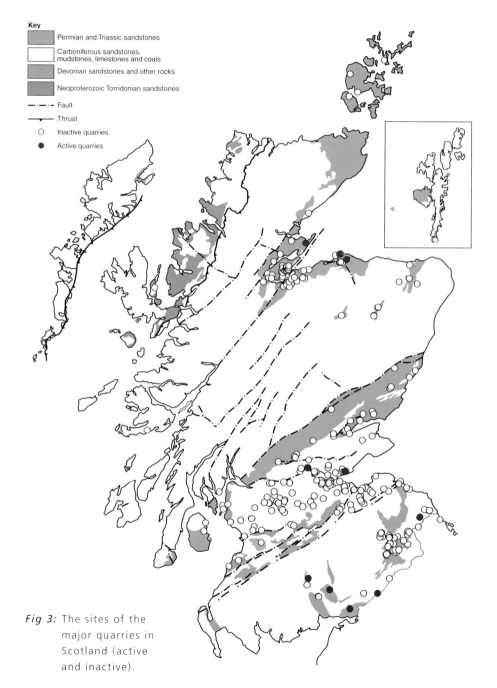

Fig 3: The sites of the major quarries in Scotland (active and inactive).

many more in this rigorous pursuit, earlier recognised for its demanding lifestyle by Robert Burns in "The Twa Dogs" but a source of inspiration to Hugh Miller in "The Old Red Sandstone" (1841). The Locharbriggs quarry alone employed 267 men by 1899. It is estimated that, at the height of this industry, 20,000 tonnes of the 'new', post-Carboniferous red sandstone (fig 2) were transported annually from these Solway sites by sea, canal and, importantly for Edinburgh, by the new railway system. The larger quarries had been linked in the 1890's to the 'Caledonian' Carlisle to Glasgow line, opened in 1847. A spur connected the Cove quarries at Kirkpatrick Fleming in 1859. Valuable red sandstone strata were also to be found in Mauchline and on the Isle of Arran but those at Moffat and Ballantrae were never quarried commercially (Boyle 1909). The most active quarries (fig 3)

(McMillan 1997) supplied the lowland belt of Scotland, yielding stone for the capital particularly from the 1880's to the early years of the 20th century. As with Glasgow and other conurbations, red sandstone lends itself to the construction of churches, schools, banks and offices, hospitals, galleries, and homes, whether tenement, terraced or singular.

Sandstone is one of the sedimentary rocks, a patient mixture of particles and cements disposed in three dimensions to give much subtlety and variation. The process of sedimentation comprises compaction, dewatering and cementation. Organisms and shells, vegetation and older rocks produce the grains which are bonded together by the precipitating crystals of minerals and water in the atmosphere. This primeval brew of air, sand and water is then compacted by pressure to deliver layered stone, the deliberate magic of lithification. Drying results in shrinkage, with additional perturbation from movement of the earth's crust. Thus form joints and stress fractures, through the bedding planes (fig 4).

Sedimentary rocks therefore possess important and characteristic properties which impart behavioural differences under load or when subjected to the decay and dissolutions of exposure (McMillan et al 1999). Colour is imparted by metals, principally the iron oxides, with aluminium and magnesium salts, lime and other elements cementing the mass of predominant quartz (silica) grains (91-98 per cent of the total volume). White and black poikilitic mottling results from particulate matter and offers further differentiations (Boyle 1909). The historical personality and age of the stone can be appreciated by the enthusiast, similarly to the rings of a tree trunk (fig 5) or the growth arrest lines in human bones (fig 6).

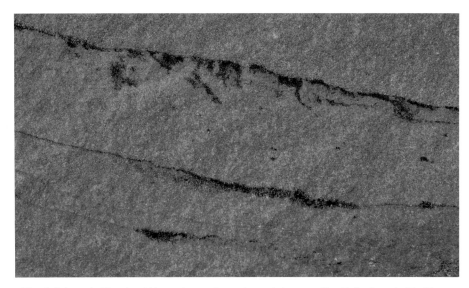

Fig 4 (above): The bedding planes in red sandstone. *Fig 5 (below left):* Rings of age in a cross-section of a fossilised tree trunk. *Fig 6 (below right):* Growth arrest lines in the femur and tibia as a result of annual winter skiing.

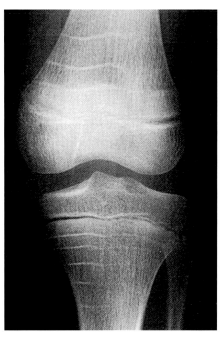

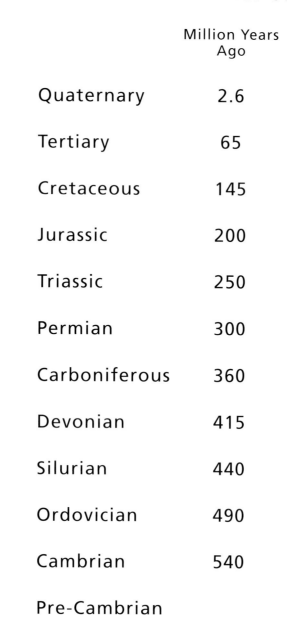

	Million Years Ago
Quaternary	2.6
Tertiary	65
Cretaceous	145
Jurassic	200
Triassic	250
Permian	300
Carboniferous	360
Devonian	415
Silurian	440
Ordovician	490
Cambrian	540
Pre-Cambrian	

Fig 8: The surface texture of Triassic stone.

Fig 9: The surface texture of Permian stone.

Fig 7: The different geological ages, including the Triassic and Permian strata.

The new red sandstone derived from the Triassic and Permian periods (fig 7), some 200 to 300 million years ago. The Triassic stone was softer (fig 8) and allowed more intricate carving by the artisans of the day. This variant was fluvial or water-lain, in that it was the product of rivers, lakes (lacustrine) and the sea, marked by currents to produce 'cross-bedding'. Sources included the Annan and Kirtle Water quarries of Corsehill and Cove, and the less known Milnfield, Redgatehead, Gallowbank, Milbie, Brydekirk, Old Warmanbie and Annan Heath quarries (Hawkins 2001).

Permian red sandstone was dune-bedded or aeolian, having been formed by the wind during the time that this region of Scotland was a desert and close to the equator, before its ultimate migration northwards. Cross-bedding is also evident, but with a greater degree of sand particle sorting and sphericity. The Permian stone (fig 9) is both older and more durable than the Triassic, much of it being quarried at Locharbriggs, Corncockle (Lochmaben), Gatelawbridge and Knowehead. Using microscopic sections (fig 10), constituent grain size and porosity can now be assayed (Hyslop 2004; Hyslop et al 2006), particularly important when considering the replacement and repair of damaged and weathered buildings. The fingerprinting of these stones is made even more precise by mineralogical and geochemical analysis. Yet in older days the stone mason and the architect alike knew and would choose from the feel and surface hardness of the different stones (Craig 1893) in a way that nowadays we can only admire.

By the time of the First World War concrete and brick were becoming dominant, especially in those areas distant from active quarries. Glass and metal have also introduced themselves to an increasing degree, yet stone

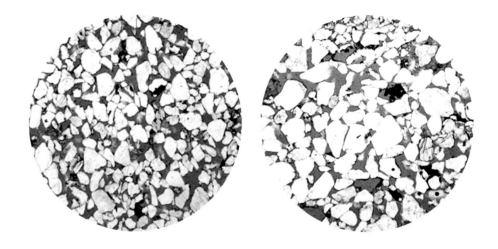

Fig 10: Microscopic sections of the two types of new red sandstone Triassic (Corsehill) left, Permian (Locharbriggs) right. Scale: 1cm = 0.8mm

still offers durability and energy conservation, coupled with acceptable maintenance costs if its upkeep is sympathetic and disciplined. In its wildest forms it will outlast us all, red sandstone providing the wonders of the Grand Canyon, Ayers Rock (Uluru), Petra in Jordan and the shifting contours of the Namib Desert.

As Edinburgh's own local quarries at Burgh Muir, Craigleith, Craigmillar, Ravelston and Redhall, Hailes, Binny, Dalmeny, Hermand, Hopetown and Humbie began to be exhausted and filled in, so did the Solway stone prove to be both architecturally attractive and readily available. Many other towns used the new red sandstone but this book celebrates only the architecture relevant to the Scottish capital. With this limited but appealing brief the authors hope that they have brought together a group of still vibrant buildings, some remarkable, some mundane.

References

Boyle, R. 'The economic and petrographic geology of the New Red Sandstones of the South and West of Scotland'. Transactions of the Geological Society of Glasgow Vol 13, pp 344-384, Glasgow, 1909.

Cant, Malcolm. Marchmont, Sciennes and the Grange. Malcolm Cant Publications, Edinburgh, 2001.

Craig, G. 'Building Stones used in Edinburgh: their Geological Sources, relative Durability and other Characteristics'. Transactions of the Edinburgh Geological Society, vol 6, Edinburgh, 1893.

Gifford, John, McWilliam, Colin and Walker, David. Edinburgh volume of The Buildings of Scotland. eds Nikolaus Pevsner and Colin McWilliam. Yale University Press in association with the Buildings of Scotland Trust, 1984, 1988, 1991.

Hawkins, James I. The Sandstone Heritage of Dumfriesshire. The Friends of Annandale and Eskdale Museums. Solway Offset Printers, Dumfries, 2001.

Hyslop, Ewan K. Research Report: 'The Performance of Replacement Sandstone in the New Town of Edinburgh'. Historic Scotland, Edinburgh, 2004.

Hyslop, Ewan, McMillan, Andrew, and Maxwell, Ingval. Stone in Scotland. British Geological Survey, UNESCO Publishing, Paris, 2006.

MacGregor, A G. The Mineral Resources of the Lothians. Geological Survey Wartime Pamphlet, No 45, Edinburgh, 1945.

McKean, Charles. Edinburgh: an Illustrated Architectural Guide. Royal Incorporation of Architects in Scotland, Edinburgh (2nd edition), 1992.

McMillan, Andrew A. 'Quarries of Scotland: an Illustrated Guide to Scottish Geology and Stone Working based on the British Geological Survey Photographic Archive of selected Building Stone Quarries'. Historic Scotland Technical Advice Note, No 12. Edinburgh. Historic Scotland, 1997.

McMillan, Andrew A, Gillanders, R J and Fairhurst, J A. Building Stones of Edinburgh. Edinburgh Geological Society (2nd edition), 1999.

Miller, Hugh. The Old Red Sandstone. W P Nimmo, Edinburgh, 1841.

Smith, Charles J. Historic South Edinburgh. Vol 2, pp 353-358. Charles Skilton Ltd, Edinburgh and London, 1979.

Youngson, A J. The Making of Classical Edinburgh. Edinburgh University Press, Edinburgh, 1966.

Exposed Old Red Sandstone (Pre-Carboniferous) near Siccar Point, Berwickshire.

Public Buildings

Above: Former Slateford District Fire Station, Angle Park Terrace (1894-1900: Robert Morham)
Opposite: Prudential Assurance building, South St Andrew Street – now Tiles bar and café (1895: Alfred Waterhouse)

Fire Station (Edinburgh Fire Brigade), Lauriston (Locharbriggs and Closeburn: 1897-1901: Robert Morham)

Fire Station (Edinburgh Fire Brigade), Lauriston (Locharbriggs and Closeburn: 1897-1901: Robert Morham)

Church Hill Theatre (converted in 1965) – formerly Morningside Free Church (Corsehill: 1892: Hippolyte J Blanc)

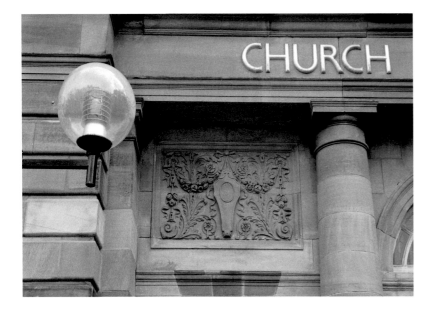

Church Hill Theatre (converted in 1965) – formerly Morningside Free Church (Corsehill: 1892: Hippolyte J Blanc)

King's Theatre, Tollcross (Closeburn [with indents of Greenhill in 1980's]: 1904: J D Swanston and James Davidson)

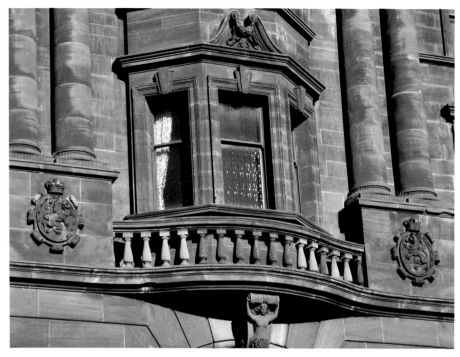

King's Theatre, Tollcross (Closeburn [with indents of Greenhill in 1980's]: 1904: J D Swanston and James Davidson)

Caledonian Hilton Hotel, West End (Locharbriggs and some Corncockle: 1890-1893 & 1899-1903: Sir George Washington Browne & J M Dick Peddie)

Caledonian Hilton Hotel, West End (Locharbriggs and some Corncockle: 1890-1893 & 1899-1903: Sir George Washington Browne & J M Dick Peddie)

Caledonian Hilton Hotel, West End (Locharbriggs and some Corncockle: 1890-1893 & 1899-1903: Sir George Washington Browne & J M Dick Peddie)

Caledonian Hilton Hotel, West End (Locharbriggs and some Corncockle: 1890-1893 & 1899-1903: Sir George Washington Browne & J M Dick Peddie)

Royal Hospital for Sick Children, Sciennes Road (Corsehill: 1892-97: Sir George Washington Browne)

Royal Hospital for Sick Children, Sciennes Road (Corsehill: 1892-97: Sir George Washington Browne)

Lothian Health Offices, Pleasance – formerly the Deaconess Hospital (1894/97: Hardy and Wight [Lady Grisell Baillie Memorial])

Lothian Health Offices, Pleasance – formerly the Deaconess Hospital
(1894/97: Hardy and Wight [Lady Grisell Baillie Memorial])

Royal Victoria Hospital bas relief of Royal Arms (c.1894)

City Hospital, Greenbank Drive – now residential (1896-1903: Robert Morham)

Royal Infirmary Diamond Jubilee Pavilion (Corsehill: 1897: Sydney Mitchell and Wilson)

Prudential Assurance building, South St Andrew Street – now Tiles bar and café (1895: Alfred Waterhouse)

Royal Bank of Scotland, Nicolson Street (Corncockle: 1902: Thomas P Marwick)

Scottish National Portrait Gallery, Queen Street (Corsehill and Moat: 1885-90: Sir Robert Rowand Anderson)

Scottish National Portrait Gallery, Queen Street (Corsehill and Moat: 1885-90: Sir Robert Rowand Anderson)

Scottish National Portrait Gallery, Queen Street (Corsehill and Moat: 1885-90: Sir Robert Rowand Anderson)

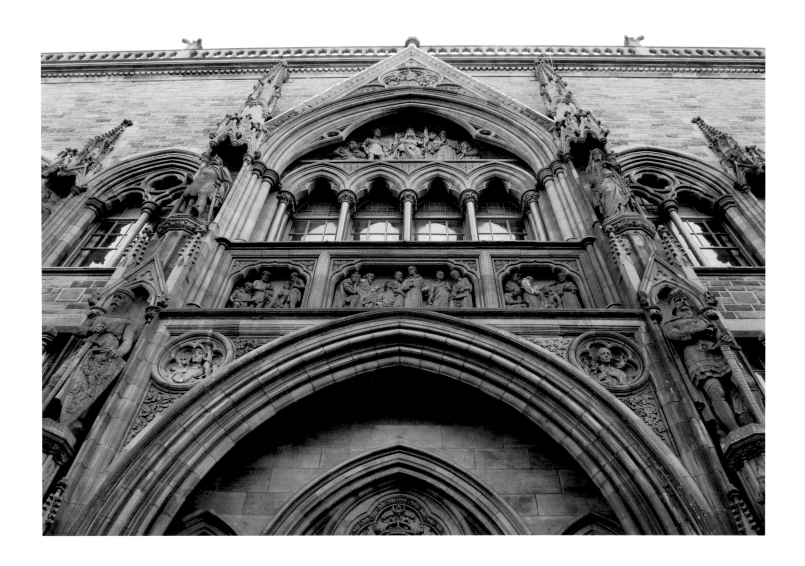

Scottish National Portrait Gallery, Queen Street (Corsehill and Moat: 1885-90: Sir Robert Rowand Anderson)

Leith Victoria Public Baths, Junction Place,
Leith (1896/9: George Simpson)

Portobello Public Baths (1898: Robert Morham)

Above: Portobello Public Baths detail
Below: Leith Victoria Public Baths detail

Jenner's Workshop, Rose Street
(Gatelawbridge: 1898: Peter L Henderson)

Menzies' Hanover Buildings, Rose Street (1929: T Forbes Maclennan)

Dewar Place derelict warehouse – formerly Electric Lighting Central Generating Station (1894/8: Robert Morham)

Above: South St Andrew Street shop and warehouse
Left: Salvation Army Hall, Hamilton Place

Braid Hills Hotel (red-dressed baronial: 1886: W Hamilton Beattie)

Churches

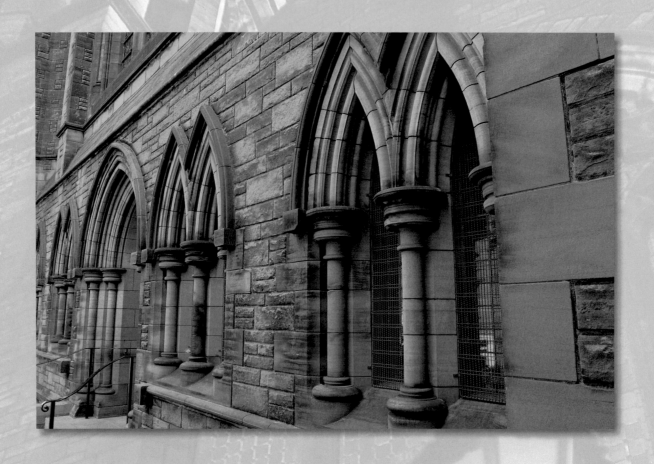

Above: Belford Hostel – formerly Dean Free Church (1888: Sydney Mitchell and Wilson)

Opposite: Morningside Parish Church – formerly St Matthew's Church

Bristo Place Seventh-Day Adventist Church (Evangelical Union) (1900: Sydney Mitchell & Wilson)

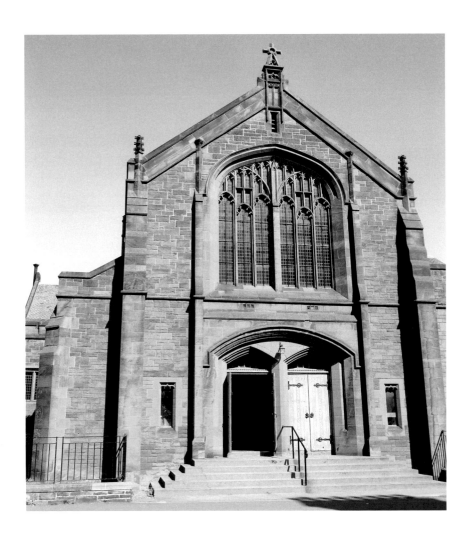

St Stephen's Church, Comely Bank
(red sandstone and neo-Perp detail:
1901: J N Scott and A Lorne Campbell)

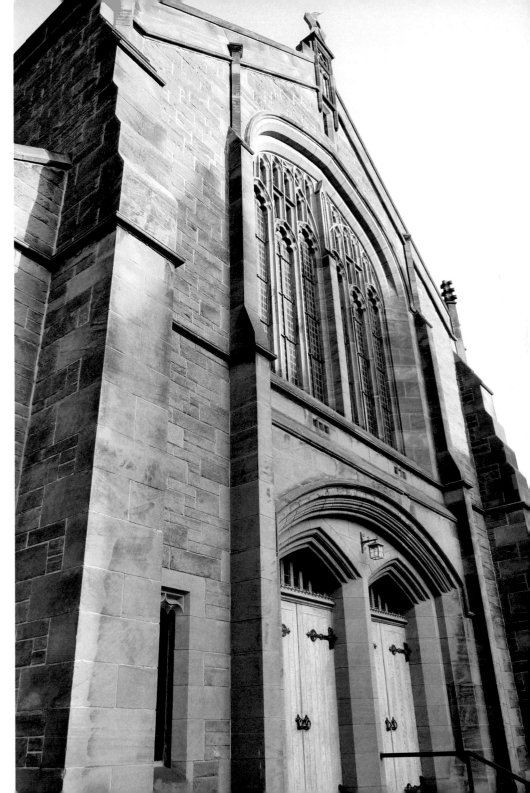

Craiglockhart Parish Church (1889 [steeple 1899]: George Henderson)

Craiglockhart Parish Church (1889 [steeple 1899]: George Henderson)

Gorgie Parish Church – formerly Cairns Memorial Church (1900/02: Robert Macfarlane Cameron [church hall: 1896: David Robertson])

Currie Presbyterian Church, Lanark Road West – formerly
Gibson Craig Memorial Hall (1900: James Macintyre Henry)

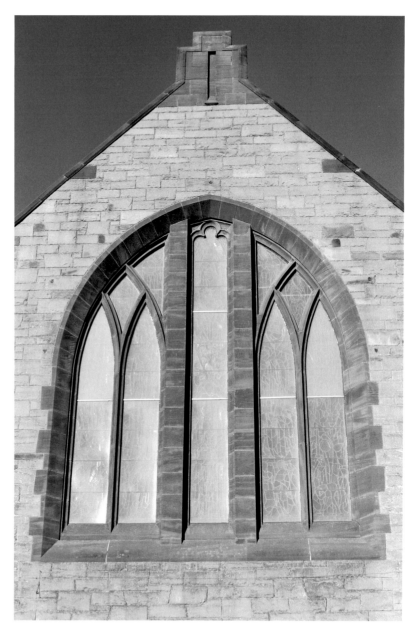

Greenbank Church – formerly Greenbank United Free Church
(Gothic with red sandstone edges: 1927: A Lorne Campbell)

Dean Parish Church (1902/3: Dunn and Findlay)

Dean Parish Church (1902/3: Dunn and Findlay)

Cluny Centre (of Morningside Parish Church) – formerly South Morningside (Braid Road) Free Church (1892: Sir Robert Rowand Anderson)

Cluny Centre (of Morningside Parish Church) – formerly South Morningside (Braid Road) Free Church (1892: Sir Robert Rowand Anderson)

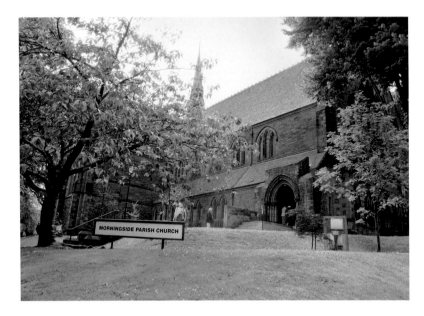

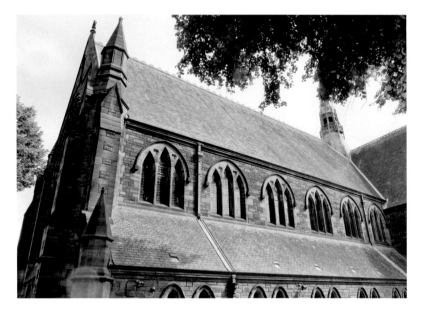

Morningside Parish Church – formerly St Matthew's Church
(uniting with South Morningside Parish Church in 1974, initially to form Cluny Parish Church [1890: Hippolyte J Blanc])

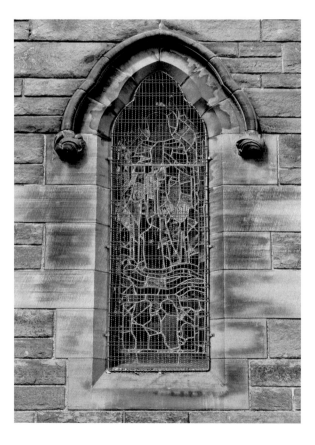

Morningside Parish Church – formerly St Matthew's Church
(uniting with South Morningside Parish Church in 1974, initially to form Cluny Parish Church [1890: Hippolyte J Blanc])

Polwarth Parish Church – formerly Candlish Church and before that Merchiston United Free Church (1898/9-1902: Sydney Mitchell)

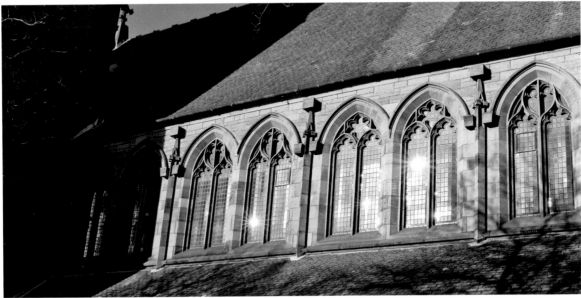

Polwarth Parish Church – formerly Candlish Church and before that Merchiston United Free Church (1898/9-1902: Sydney Mitchell)

Polwarth Parish Church – formerly Candlish Church and before that Merchiston United Free Church (1898/9-1902: Sydney Mitchell)

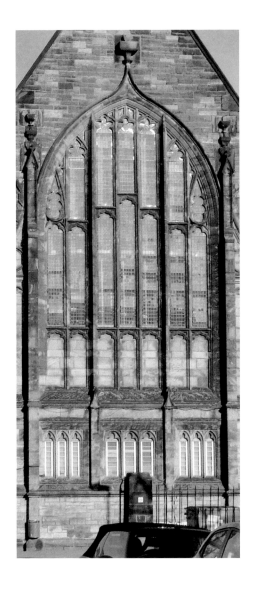

St Margaret's School Hall – formerly Craigmillar Park Free Church (1898: Sydney Mitchell and Wilson)

St Cuthbert's Episcopal Church, Colinton (1888/9: Sir Robert Rowand Anderson [north east tower built in 1893: south transept in 1899: re-opened in1898])

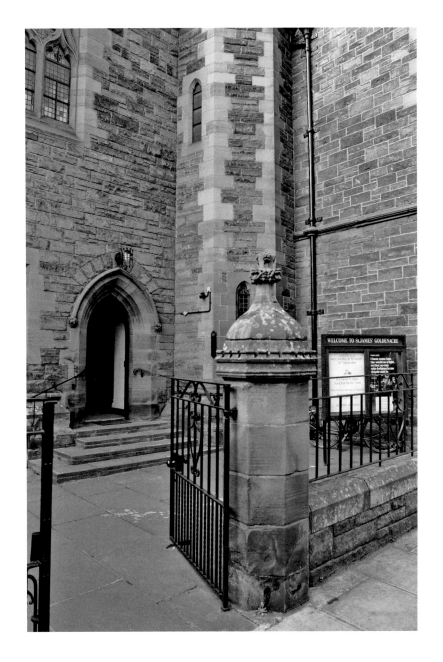

St James Episcopal Church, Inverleith Row (Corsehill: 1885: Sir Robert Rowand Anderson)

St Serf's Church, Ferry and Clark Roads (1901: G Mackie Watson [chancel built in 1925])

Warrender Park Free Church, Whitehouse Loan – now residential (red sandstone Rennaisance with pedimented centrepiece: 1891: R M Cameron)

Schools & Libraries

Above: Scotch Whisky Heritage Centre – formerly Castlehill School (Hailes and Corncockle: 1888 / 1896: Robert Wilson)
Opposite: High Street Primary School, Canongate – formerly Milton House School (Corncockle with Hailes: 1886: Robert Wilson)

High Street Primary School, Canongate – formerly Milton House School (Corncockle with Hailes: 1886: Robert Wilson)

Bruntsfield Primary School (1893: Robert Wilson [and latterly John A Carfrae])

Roseburn Primary School (Hailes and Corsehill: 1893: Robert Wilson)

South Morningside Primary School, Comiston Road (1891: Robert Wilson)

Corner House Day Nursery, South Gillsland Road (1897: Frank Simon)

Stockbridge Library, Hamilton Place – formerly a school (1898/1900: H Ramsay Taylor)

Currie Library – formerly Currie School, Lanark Road West (1903: William Baillie)

Solicitors' Building (Library), High Street (1898: James B Dunn) and the Cowgate Tourist Hostel below

Edinburgh College of Art, Lauriston (Locharbriggs and Closeburn: 1906/10: J M Dick Peddie)

Edinburgh College of Art, Lauriston (Locharbriggs and Closeburn: 1906/10: J M Dick Peddie)

Edinburgh College of Art, Lauriston
(Locharbriggs and Closeburn: 1906/10: J M Dick Peddie: [Hunter Building in Locharbriggs stone: 1972: W Anthony Wheeler])

Edinburgh College of Art, Lauriston (Locharbriggs and Closeburn: 1906/10: J M Dick Peddie)

Public Houses

Golf Tavern, Bruntsfield Links (1899: R M Cameron)

Abbotsford Bar, Rose Street (Gatelawbridge: 1902: Peter L Henderson)

Left: Robertsons 37 Bar, Rose Street (Gatelawbridge: 1898: Peter L Henderson)
Centre: Athletic Arms, Angle Park Terrace, Gorgie (1882)   *Right:* Greenmantle Bar, Nicolson Street

Rosekeith Café and Bar, Coburg and Quayside Roads, Leith (c.1900)

Left: Hermitage Bar – now re-named Morning Glory (part of giant red sandstone Rennaissance block: 1889: W Hamilton Beattie)
Right: Princes Street (no 70) – formerly the Edinburgh Café (Corsehill: 1886: Hippolyte J Blanc)

Homes

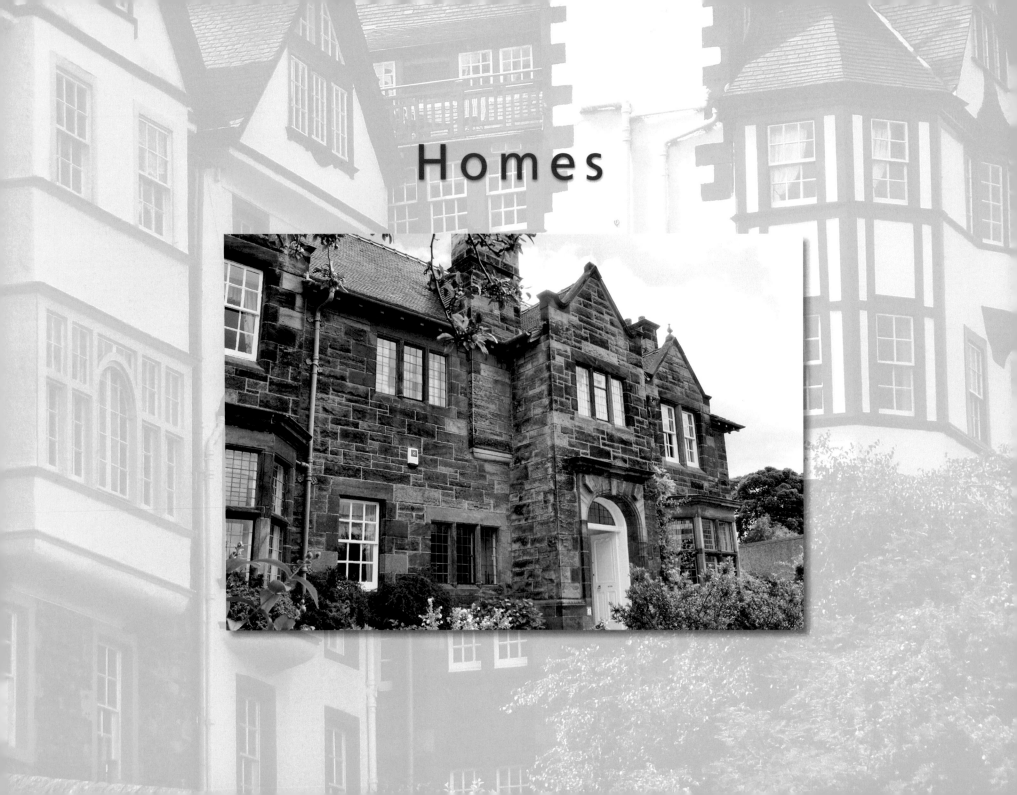

Above: Braid Avenue house (1888: Wardrop & Anderson)
Opposite: Red House, South Gillsland Road (1897: Frank Simon)

Dean Village – formerly Water of Leith Village (rust-tinted rubble with droved freestone dressings:
1120's onwards: wheatsheaf roundel: 1805: Well Court: 1883/6: Sydney Mitchell: Hawthorn Buildings: 1895: Dunn and Findlay)

Dean Village – formerly Water of Leith Village (rust-tinted rubble with droved freestone dressings:
1120's onwards: wheatsheaf roundel: 1805: Well Court: 1883/6: Sydney Mitchell: Hawthorn Buildings: 1895: Dunn and Findlay)

Dean Village – formerly Water of Leith Village (rust-tinted rubble with droved freestone dressings:
1120's onwards: wheatsheaf roundel: 1805: Well Court: 1883/6: Sydney Mitchell: Hawthorn Buildings: 1895: Dunn and Findlay)

Dean Village – formerly Water of Leith Village (rust-tinted rubble with droved freestone dressings:
1120's onwards: wheatsheaf roundel: 1805: Well Court: 1883/6: Sydney Mitchell: Hawthorn Buildings: 1895: Dunn and Findlay)

Canaan Grove, Newbattle Terrace (c.1884)

Left: Lanark Road mansion

Top Right: Cardon, Mortonhall Road (1902: Thomas T Paterson)   *Bottom Right:* Cuddies Lane corner house, Colinton Village

Polwarth Terrace houses, (1900: Sydney Mitchell and Wilson)

Left: Colinton Road house (1897: Frank Simon)
Top and Bottom Right: Redcliffe, Succoth Place

Red House, South Gillsland Road (1897: Frank Simon)

Red House, South Gillsland Road (1897: Frank Simon)

Inverleith Place house – (pink Corncockle and red Locharbriggs: 1899)

Inverleith Place houses – (pink Corncockle and red Locharbriggs: 1899)

Left: Braid Avenue house   *Top Right:* Roseburn Cliff houses
Bottom Centre: Portobello tenements (1893-1896)   *Bottom Right:* Gatepost Pillar, Colinton Road

Morningside Park houses (c.1870: Pilkington & Bell)

Left: Mid Gillsland Road house   *Right:* Cluny Gardens house
Centre: Braid Crescent house (c.1887: Sir George Washington Browne)

Windsor Mansions, Portobello (1895/6: Edward Calvert, John Baxter & Robert Brown)

Gifford Park and Buccleuch Street tenement (1887)

Harrison Road tenement (1900: Sydney Mitchell & Wilson)

Above: Lanark Road tenement and beauty parlour (1904)
Below: Boroughloch tenement, Meadows

Above: High Street tenements   *Below:* Tollcross tenement
and Italian restaurant, Ponton Street and Viewforth

Left: Leith tenement, Duke and Academy Streets (1898)   *Top:* Leith tenement, North Junction Street and Ferry Road (1901)
Centre: Leith tenement, King Street (1905)   *Right:* Leith tenement, North Junction Street and Admiralty Street

Left: Leith tenement, Ferry and Newhaven Roads
Centre: Leith tenement, Shore Place (1898: J W Maclean)　　*Right:* Leith tenement, Henderson Street (1891: James Simpson)

Left and Right: West Port tenements and shops (1887 and 1878)

Polwarth Crescent and Merchiston Avenue tenement
(1896/7: James M Thomson)

Leith tenement, Henderson Street (1898: James Simpson)

Ramsay Garden – formerly Allan Ramsay House c.1740 but with extensions (1892: S Henbest Capper: 1893/4: Sydney Mitchell)

Ramsay Garden – formerly Allan Ramsay House c.1740 but with extensions (1892: S Henbest Capper: 1893/4: Sydney Mitchell)

Ramsay Garden – formerly Allan Ramsay House c.1740 but with extensions (1892: S Henbest Capper: 1893/4: Sydney Mitchell)

Ramsay Garden – formerly Allan Ramsay House c.1740 but with extensions (1892: S Henbest Capper: 1893/4: Sydney Mitchell)

Architectural Details

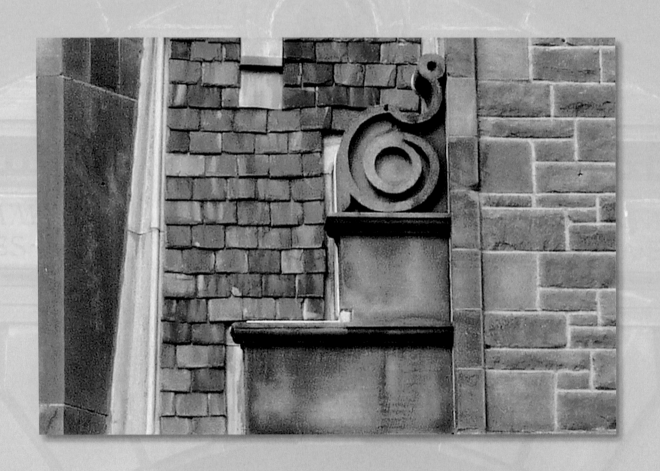

Left & Centre: Drumsheugh Toll, Belford Road (1891: Sir George Washington Browne)   *Right:* Sir William Fraser Homes, 52 Spylaw Bank Road (1898/9: A F Balfour Paul)   *Opposite:* Windsor Mansions, Portobello (1895/6: Edward Calvert, John Baxter & Robert Brown)

Meadows Sundial (Corncockle and Moat: 1886: James Cowan)

Meadows Commemorative Pillars (Corncockle, Corsehill, Gatelawbridge and Moat: 1886: James Gowans)

Colinton Bridge, Colinton Village (1874)

Above: St Ninian's Centre, The Pleasance
Below: Bruntsfield Primary School

Above: Craiglockhart Parish Church
Below: Belford Hostel – formerly Dean Free Church

Observatory Road [Harrison] Memorial Arch (1887/8: Sydney Mitchell)

Inverleith Memorial Arch, Inverleith Park (1891: Sydney Mitchell)

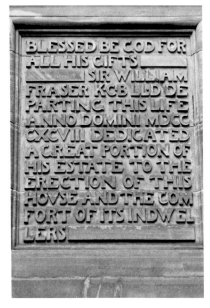

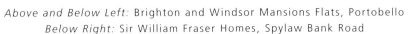
Above and Below Left: Brighton and Windsor Mansions Flats, Portobello
Below Right: Sir William Fraser Homes, Spylaw Bank Road

Above Left: Leith tenement, Henderson Street
Above Right: Well Court, Dean Village   *Below:* Roseburn Cliff house

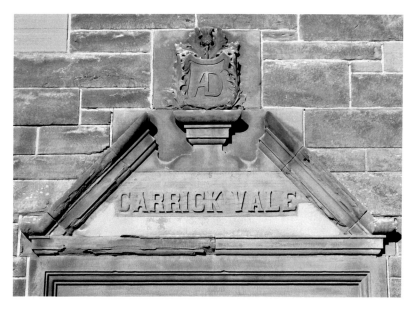

Above: Morningside Park House
Below: Lady Stairs Close, Lawnmarket

Above: Carrick Vale, Balgreen Road
Below: Cordiner's Land, West Port

Above Left: Sir William Fraser Homes, Spylaw Bank Road   *Below Left*: Pillar, Craigleith Road   *Centre:* Fountain at Portobello Promenade
Above Right: Salvation Army Women's Hostel, West Port (1910: John Hamilton)   *Below Right:* Tivoli Cinema, Gorgie (1933: John McKissack & Sons)

Meadows Sundial (Corncockle and Moat: 1886: James Cowan)

Index of Illustrations

This list cannot be comprehensive as space does not permit the inclusion of many of the houses, smaller tenements, walls and indents that flourish in red sandstone. The index and captions are listed in the following order: Property: (Quarry: Date: Architect). Where the provenance of the stone is uncertain quarry details are excluded.

Additional Buildings of Interest (Not Illustrated)

Blackford Avenue, Maurice Place (1897) and Eva Place (1902)

Boroughmuir School Annexe, Warrender Park Crescent (1902: John A Carfrae)

Boroughmuir School Annexe, Bruntsfield – formerly St Oswald Church and before that St Mark Church (1894: Henry F Kerr)

Braeburn, 35 Inverleith Terrace (1895: Thomas T Paterson)

Chesser Avenue terraced houses and tenement

Couper Street School, Leith (1889/90: George Craig)

East Broughton Place Church Hall (Corsehill dressings:1887)

Ferry Road terraced houses (1890's)

Foot of the Walk Pub, Leith Walk, Constitution and Duke Streets

The Gair, Lanark Road (1904: Edward C H Maidman) and red sandstone houses continuing westwards

- INDEX -

ACKNOWLEDGEMENTS

The authors warmly thank:

Colin Baxter	*Malcolm Cant*
Jim Hawkins	*Ewan Hyslop*
Julianne Irvine	*Charles McKean*
Andrew McMillan	*Mike Rensner*

Their expertise and enthusiastic support ensured that the production of this book was a most enjoyable and stimulating experience. Annie Macnicol has been central to the project, enlivening our efforts with the provision of photographs and her commentary about the developing text.

Published in Great Britain in 2009 by
Malcolm Macnicol, Red House, South Gillsland Road, Edinburgh EH10 5DE, Scotland

Text © Malcolm Macnicol & Michael Devlin 2009
Foreword © Andrew McMillan 2009

Photographs © 2009 by:
Michael Devlin © front cover, pages: 2, 6tl, 7t, 8, 14, 15, 16, 17, 18, 19, 20, 21, 22, 23, 24, 25tl, 25r, 29, 31, 32, 33, 34, 35, 39, 41, 42, 43, 44tr, 44br, 47, 48tl, 48bl, 49r, 50, 51tr, 52tr, 53, 54, 55l, 57b, 59, 61, 64, 65t, 65br, 66, 67, 68, 73, 74, 75, 76t, 76br, 77, 78, 79, 83l, 84, 88, 94t, 94bc, 95, 106l, 109l, 110tl, 110bl, 114, 115l, 115r, 117, 118, 123.
Annie Macnicol © back cover, pages 7bl, 11, 44l, 46, 51l, 51br, 52tl, 52br, 55r, 56, 58, 60tl, 65bl, 85, 86c, 86tr, 89, 92, 93, 94bl, 94br, 96, 97tl, 98l, 98tr, 98br, 101, 109r, 110bc, 110r, 111, 112, 116, 120br, 122c.

Malcolm Macnicol © pages 7br, 12, 13, 25bl, 26, 27, 28, 30, 36, 37, 38, 40, 45, 48r, 49l, 52bl, 55c, 57tl 57tr 60bl, 60bc, 60r, 62, 63, 69, 70, 71, 72, 76bl, 80, 81, 82, 83r, 86tl, 86cl, 86bl, 86cr, 86br, 87, 90, 91, 97bl, 97r, 98bc, 99, 100, 102, 103, 104, 105, 106r, 107, 108, 113, 119, 120tl, 120tc, 120tr, 120bl, 120bc, 121, 122tl, 122bl, 122tr, 122br, 128.
A A McMillan © page 4.
Reproduced by permission of the **British Geoglogical Survey** © NERC.
All rights reserved. IPR/114-67CT: pages 6r, 9, 115c

A CIP Catalogue record for this book is available from the British Library.
ISBN 978-1-84107-453-5   Printed in China

Front cover: Top: Scottish National Portrait Gallery, Royal Hospital for Sick Children Armorial Arch, Edinburgh College of Art.   **Bottom:** Caledonian Hilton Hotel, The Golf Tavern, Fire Station (EFB).
Back cover: Solicitors' Building (Library).   **Page 2:** Locharbriggs Quarry.   **Page 128:** Detail from Red House, South Gillsland Road.